# Assessment of Estuarine Water and Sediment Quality at Cape Lookout and Cape Hatteras National Seashores, 2010

Natural Resource Data Series NPS/SECN/NRDS—2011/179

M. Brian Gregory

National Park Service
Southeast Coast Inventory and Monitoring Network
160 Phoenix Road
Athens, GA 30605


Katy Austin Smith

University of Georgia
Marine Extension Service
715 Bay Street
Brunswick, GA 31520

July 2011

U.S. Department of the Interior
National Park Service
Natural Resource Stewardship and Science
Fort Collins, Colorado

The National Park Service, Natural Resource Stewardship and Science office in Fort Collins, Colorado publishes a range of reports that address natural resource topics of interest and applicability to a broad audience in the National Park Service and others in natural resource management, including scientists, conservation and environmental constituencies, and the public.

The Natural Resource Data Series is intended for the timely release of basic data sets and data summaries. Care has been taken to assure accuracy of raw data values, but a thorough analysis and interpretation of the data has not been completed. Consequently, the initial analyses of data in this report are provisional and subject to change.

All manuscripts in the series receive the appropriate level of peer review to ensure that the information is scientifically credible, technically accurate, appropriately written for the intended audience, and designed and published in a professional manner.

Data in this report were collected and analyzed using methods based on established, peer-reviewed protocols and were analyzed and interpreted within the guidelines of the protocols.

Views, statements, findings, conclusions, recommendations, and data in this report do not necessarily reflect views and policies of the National Park Service, U.S. Department of the Interior. Mention of trade names or commercial products does not constitute endorsement or recommendation for use by the U.S. Government.

This report is available from the Southeast Coast Network (http://science.nature.nps.gov/im/units/secn) and the Natural Resource Publications Management website (http://www.nature.nps.gov/publications/nrpm/)

Please cite this publication as:

Gregory, M. Brian, and K. A. Smith. 2011. Assessment of estuarine water and sediment quality at Cape Lookout and Cape Hatteras National Seashores, 2010. Natural Resource Data SeriesNPS/SECN/NRDS—2011/179. National Park Service, Fort Collins, Colorado.

NPS 603/108715, 623/108715, July2011

# Contents

                                                                                    Page

Contents ....................................................................................................... iii

Summary and Key Findings......................................................................... v

Introduction................................................................................................... 1

    Cape Lookout............................................................................................ 2

    Cape Hatteras........................................................................................... 2

Methods......................................................................................................... 5

    Site Selection ........................................................................................... 5

    Water-Quality Data Collection ............................................................... 6

    Water-Quality Assessment Criteria ........................................................ 6

    Sediment Data Collection ........................................................................ 7

    Sediment Assessment Criteria ................................................................ 7

Water-Quality Condition Assessments ........................................................ 11

Sediment Condition Assessments ................................................................ 17

Water-Quality Data...................................................................................... 21

Sediment-Quality Data................................................................................. 23

Literature Cited ........................................................................................... 27

# Summary and Key Findings

1. In July 2010, the Southeast Coast Network and the University of Georgia conducted an assessment of water- and sediment-quality at Cape Lookout and Cape Hatteras National Seashores as a part of the NPS Vital Signs Monitoring Program.

2. Monitoring was conducted following methods developed by the U.S. Environmental Protection Agency as a part of the National Coastal Assessment Program and included laboratory analysis for chlorophyll *a*, total dissolved nitrogen (TDN) and phosphorous concentrations and field measurements of water temperature, pH, dissolved oxygen, and salinity. Estimates of water-clarity were made using secchi depth measurements and were adjusted for naturally occurring water-clarity conditions.

3. Overall water-quality at the park ranged from *fair* to *poor* with the majority of sites found to be in *fair* condition (83%); only one site rated as *poor*.

4. Nitrogen levels were at concentrations considered *fair* at 77 %of sites although *poor* conditions were noted at the remaining sites. Phosphorus concentrations were generally *fair to good*. Only a single site located just north of the Cape Hatteras Lighthouse rated *poor* due to elevated phosphorus levels.

5. Chlorophyll *a* and dissolved oxygen levels were *good* throughout the parks; only 13% of sites rated in the *fair* range for chlorophyll *a* and only 3% rated as *fair* for dissolved oxygen.

6. Overall sediment conditions were considered *good* at all sites sampled showing only trace amounts of metals and little or no organic contamination.

7. Higher levels of nutrients, especially TDN, were more common in the parks' northern waters potentially due to higher human population densities in this area. Continued monitoring of nutrient levels in park waters, particularly in high use areas, should be considered.

# Introduction

Estuaries are semi-enclosed coastal bodies of water that have free connection with the open sea and within which sea water mixes with fresh water. A key defining feature of an estuary is that it is an interface between sea water and fresh water and there is an influence of the ocean tide creating a dynamic relationship between the two waters. Estuaries contain critical habitat for a variety of fish and wildlife species. They serve as nursery habitats for fish, crustaceans, and shellfish and foraging habitat for birds and mammals. Additionally, they provide a multitude of recreational opportunities including boating, fishing, and bird watching. These are fragile ecosystems vulnerable to impacts caused by development and many other uses. Urban and industrial development has been shown to negatively impact estuaries severely by altering hydrodynamic processes, increasing exposure to levels of chemical contaminants that cause mortality, altered growth, and reduced reproduction of aquatic life, and increased exposure to more frequent and severe hypoxia (Lerberg et al. 2000). When nutrients from various sources, such as sewage and fertilizers, are introduced into an estuary, the concentration of available nutrients will increase beyond natural background levels. This unnatural increase in the rate of supply of organic matter is called eutrophication, which may result in a host of undesirable water-quality conditions. Excess nutrients can lead to excess plant production, and thus, to increased chlorophyll, which can decrease water-clarity and lower concentrations of dissolved oxygen. In addition, macrobenthic communities in impacted areas are often characterized by low diversity, low numbers of rare and pollution sensitive species, and low abundances (Lerberg et al. 2000). In areas with increased impervious cover, stormwater runoff is flashier and occurs in greater volumes than in undeveloped areas. This unnatural runoff can often be polluted with a wide variety of low-level contaminants that are released into estuaries and can accumulate in sediment (Holland et al. 2004).

A wide variety of metals and organic substances, such as polycyclic aromatic hydrocarbons (PAHs), polychlorinated biphenyls (PCBs), and pesticides, are discharged into estuaries from urban, agricultural, and industrial sources in the watershed. The contaminants adsorb onto suspended particles and eventually accumulate in depositional basins where they can disrupt the benthic community of invertebrates, shellfish, and crustaceans that live in or on the sediments. To the extent that the contaminants become concentrated in the organisms, they pose a risk to organisms throughout the food web—including humans.

Several factors influence the extent and severity of contamination. Fine-grained, organic-rich sediments are likely to become resuspended and transported to distant locations and are also efficient at scavenging pollutants. Thus, silty sediments high in total organic carbon (TOC) are potential sources of contamination. Conversely, organic-rich particles bind some toxicants so strongly that the threat to organisms can be greatly reduced

Cape Lookout and Cape Hatteras National Seashores are adjacently located and separately maintained park units along the Outer Banks of the North Carolina coast stretching from Beaufort Inlet on the south to

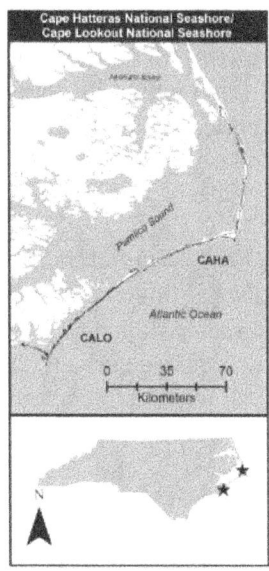

**Figure 1.** Location of Cape Lookout and Cape Hatteras National Seashores in North Carolina.

Bodie Island on the north. Together these parks encompass over 59,000 acres of beaches, upland maritime forests, tidal creeks and salt marshes. Cape Lookout and Cape Hatteras National Seashores (CALOCAHA) share a common geological history and are composed of a chain of transgressive and regressive barrier islands, formed during the Pleistocene glacial period from a large dune ridge which was located east of the Outer Bank's current location. The dune ridge gradually migrated westward during the Holocene as sea levels rose until approximately 4000 years ago when wind, waves, and currents formed the present configuration of islands. All of these islands are subject to periodic inlet formation, migration, closure, and seawater overwash during severe storms (Mallin et al. 2004).

## Cape Lookout National Seashore

Cape Lookout National Seashore includes approximately 24,500 acres of land and is composed of two main islands known as Core Banks and Shackleford Banks (Figure 1). Cape Lookout National Seashore was authorized in 1966 and transferred to the National Park Service in 1976. Presently, its two main islands are solely used for recreational purposes. Shackleford Banks has no vehicle traffic and human use of the island consists of sport fishing, swimming, surfing, hiking, camping, and nature study. Core Banks supports these same activities, but vehicle traffic is permitted along the beaches and there are some dirt roads in the interior of the islands.

Cape Lookout is bordered to the east and south by marine waters of the Atlantic Ocean. To the north and west of the Seashore are the waters of Ocracoke Inlet, Pamlico Sound, Core Sound, and Back Sound, which are polyhaline to marine in terms of salinity. Some of the coves and tidal creeks on the sound side of the park may be of variable estuarine salinities, depending on local rainfall. Hunting, primarily for waterfowl, is also permitted in the Park except within the Portsmouth Village and Cape Lookout Village historic districts (Mallin et al. 2004).

The nearby coastal ocean and sound waters are heavily utilized by commercial fishermen as well as sport fishermen. Recreational fishermen employ both angling from boats and surf fishing along this seashore. Commercial fishermen utilize pound nets to target flounder, and trawl for shrimp and finfish. Menhaden are harvested by haul seine off the ocean beach and sometimes in the sounds. Clam kicking (using outboard motors) and hydraulic dredging methods are used to harvest shellfish in the sound and have been shown to significantly reduce seagrass biomass and increase turbidity, although statistically significant reductions in bay scallop recruitment or pink shrimp abundance have not been documented in areas open to these types of mechanical harvest (Freeman 1988).

Major potential threats to water-quality near Core and Shackleford Banks include two facilities discharging approximately 4.5 mgd of treated effluent into Taylors Creek (Mallin et al. 2004) located several kilometers from the Seashore. Nonpoint pollution is not thought to be a problem due to the lack of large urban areas or concentrated livestock. Previous data collected from the western portion of Back and Core Sounds show waters that contain low average nitrate-N and moderate total phosphorus (TP) concentrations (Mallin et al. 2004).

## Cape Hatteras National Seashore

Cape Hatteras National Seashore contains 35,400 acres of land, and includes a series of barrier islands known as Bodie Island, Hatteras Island, and Ocracoke Island (Figure 1). The establishment of Cape Hatteras National Seashore was authorized in 1937 and was officially designated a National Seashore in 1953. Presently, the towns adjacent to the Seashore receive heavy seasonal usage by vacationers utilizing hotels, campgrounds, and rental homes, and there are numerous second homes owned by out of town and out of state users. There is also a seasonal flux in population, with summer populations tripling those of winter populations due to vacationers and seasonal users. This is important in terms of nutrient and fecal bacteria loads on groundwater, because all sewage on the islands is treated by septic systems (Mallin et al. 2004).

Sport fishing boats launch from Oregon and Hatteras Inlets and travel to Gulf Stream waters where trophy fish such as white marlin, blue marlin, sailfish and bluefin tuna are caught, along with the more commonly caught yellowfin tuna and dolphin. Commercial fishermen utilize pound nets to target flounder, and trawl for shrimp and finfish. Menhaden are harvested by haul seine off the ocean beach and sometimes in the sounds. Oyster production is considered to be poor and clam production is considered to be fair in the Hatteras Island area, with overall shellfishing commercial value rated as poor (Mallin et al. 2004).

Previous research has documented potential nutrient and pathogen problems near Bodie Island near Nags Head. The waters of Pamlico Sound near Hatteras Island and adjoining municipal areas that drain into the sound are potential areas for nutrient and bacterial pathogen loading and algal blooms (Mallin et al. 2004). At Ocracoke Island, the waters of Pamlico Sound, at least in areas remote from local and mainland nutrient sources are not likely to have algal blooms. However, there is an area 400 ft offshore that receives effluent from a reverse osmosis drinking water plant, effluent that has nitrogen concentrations exceeding 5 mg/L.

In July 2010, the Southeast Coast Network Inventory and Monitoring Program in cooperation with the University of Georgia conducted an assessment of water and sediment quality at Cape Lookout and Cape Hatteras National Seashores as a part of the Network's Vital Signs Monitoring program (DeVivo et al. 2008). The purpose of this document is to report the most recently collected data from within the park as part of an ongoing long-term water-quality monitoring program. This report has been designed to provide the water-quality monitoring data to managers in a concise summary format in the context of applicable federal standards that were developed by the U.S. EPA. Other data collected during this survey are available at (http://www.nature.nps.gov/publications/NRPM).

# Methods

Water-quality assessment was conducted in estuarine and tidal creek waters following the methods developed by the Environmental Protection Agency's National Coastal Assessment Program (U.S. EPA 2001). Descriptions of the water-quality parameters and the assessment criteria are from EPA's National Coastal Assessment II Report (2005). Methods suggested for use in these protocols were adapted in part and integrated into protocols tailored specifically for parks in the Southeast Coast Network (Devivo and others, *in review*). Site selection and sampling methodology are briefly outlined in the following sections.

## Site Selection

Thirty sites within the boundaries of Cape Lookout and Cape Hatteras National Seashores were randomly selected for monitoring following methods developed by the U.S. EPA (Stevens 1997, Stevens and Olsen 1999, Stevens and Olsen 2004; Figure 2). A pool of alternate sites was also selected to use if any of the original sites were not accessible. This method of randomly selecting sites in a spatially balanced manner provides managers with a statistically valid estimate of the overall conditions of assessed resources within or around the park.

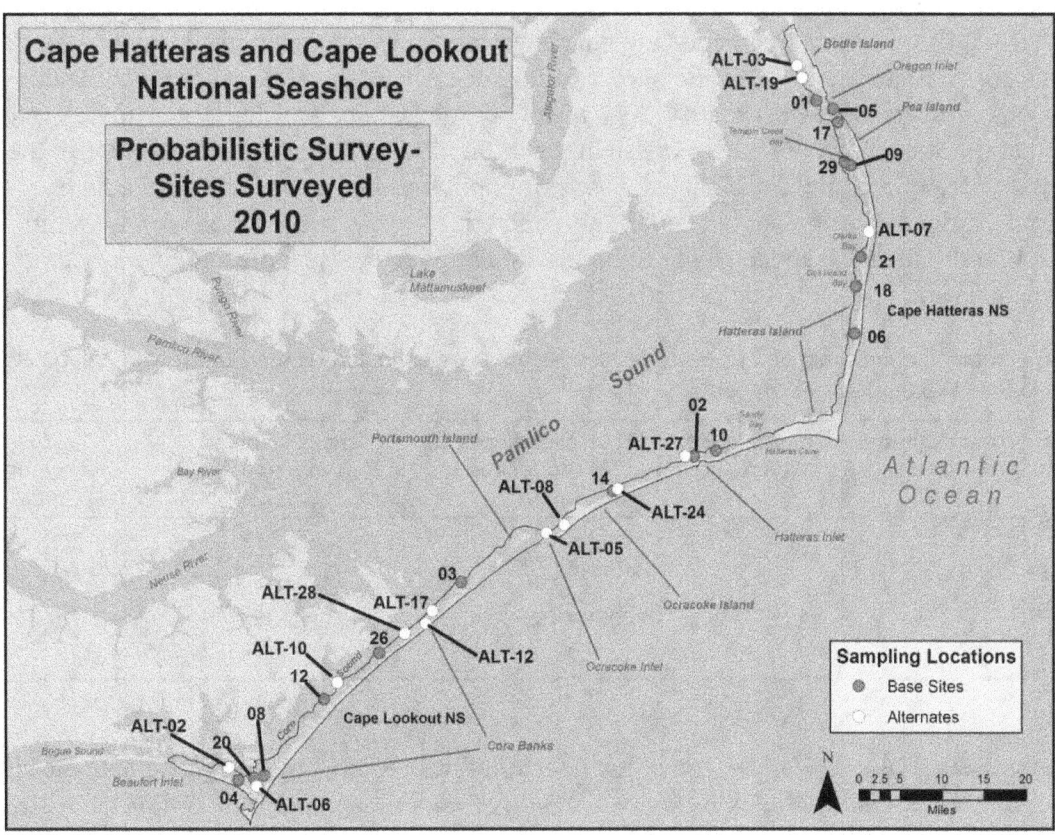

**Figure 2.** Location map showing sites sampled at Cape Lookout and Cape Hatteras National Seashores during July 2010.

## Water-Quality Data Collection

The water-quality assessment during this survey period included conducting hydrographic profiles from 0.5 to 1.0 m intervals at each site for temperature, pH, dissolved oxygen, and salinity. Only parameter values with specific water-quality criteria are presented in this report although the entire data set is available at (http://www.nature.nps.gov/publications/NRPM).

Concurrent measurements of chlorophyll *a* levels were made with nutrient samples at the surface, mid, and bottom depths, depending on total water depths, by filtering known volumes onto glass fiber filters. Filters and water samples were frozen and submitted for laboratory analysis. Shallow water sites (< 1m) were assessed using only one surface sample. Estimates of water-clarity were made at each site using a secchi disk to estimate light extinction depth which were converted to light attenuation coefficients corrected for naturally occurring turbidity conditions (Smith et al. 2006). Water clarity was not assessed at sites too shallow to ascertain an accurate secchi depth measurement. When sites were too shallow to access by boat, alternate sites were used.

## Water-Quality Assessment Criteria

Water-quality was assessed for each of the parameters following the East / Gulf Coast site criteria in EPA's National Coastal Assessment II Report (2005). The categorical assessments (i.e., *good, fair, and poor*) use measurements of chlorophyll *a*, nutrients, dissolved oxygen and water clarity (Table 1) and are intended to characterize acutely degraded water-quality conditions and does not consistently identify sites experiencing occasional or infrequent hypoxia, nutrient enrichment, or decreased water-clarity. As a result, a rating of *poor* for the water-quality index means that the site is likely to have consistently exhibited *poor* conditions before or after the assessment period. If a site is designated as *fair* or *good*, the site did not experience *poor* conditions on the date sampled, but could be characterized by *poor* conditions for short time periods. In order to assess the level of variability in the index at a specific site, increased or supplemental sampling would be needed.

**Table 1.** Condition criteria applied to water-quality parameters collected by the Southeast Coast Network during Coastal Water Quality assessment.

| Rating | Water Clarity Index (WCI) | Chlorophyll *a* (ug/L) | Total Dissolved Nitrogen (mg/L) | Total Dissolved Phosphorus (mg/L) | Dissolved Oxygen (mg/L) |
|---|---|---|---|---|---|
| Good | < 2.3 | < 5 | < 0.1 | < 0.01 | > 5 |
| Fair | 2.3 – 2.99 | 5 – 20 | 0.1 – 0.5 | 0.01 – 0.05 | 2 – 5 |
| Poor | > 3.00 | > 20 | > 0.5 | > 0.05 | < 2 |
| Missing | | | | | |

Assessments were also made using an index that combines ratings given to each parameter into a site-specific Water-Quality Index Rating which allows general comparisons between sites within a park as well as overall park conditions (Table 2). This rating allows general comparisons between parks using the percentage of sites that fall within the *good, fair* or *poor* categories.

**Table 2.** Condition criteria used for water-quality assessment summaries at individual sampling sites and park.

| Rating | Site Water-Quality Index Rating | Park Water-Quality Index Rating |
|---|---|---|
| Good | A maximum of one indicator is fair, and no indicators are poor. | Less than 10% of sites are in poor condition and less than 50% of sites are in combined poor and fair condition. |
| Fair | One of the indicators is rated poor, or two or more indicators are rated fair. | 10% to 20% of sites are in poor condition, or more than 50% of sites are in combined fair and poor condition |
| Poor | Two or more of the five indicators are rated poor. | More than 20% of sites are in poor condition |
| Missing | Two components of the indicator are missing and the available indicators do not suggest a fair or poor rating | |

## Sediment Data Collection

Assessments of sediment-quality are used to indicate the potential for sediment contaminants to affect bottom-dwelling organisms. Sediment samples were collected by taking multiple grabs at each site using a Van Veen sampler. The top 2–3 cm from each sample were composited and split in to three separate samples that were analyzed for organic contaminants, metals, total organic carbon (TOC), and grain size. If seagrasses were present at sampling locations, sediment collections were not made.

## Sediment Assessment Criteria

There are no absolute chemical concentrations that correspond to sediment toxicity, but Effects Range Low (ERL) and Effects Range Median (ERM) values are used as guidelines in assessing sediment contamination (Table 3; Long et al. 1995). ERM is the median concentration of a contaminant observed to have adverse biological effects in the literature studies examined. A more protective indicator of contaminant concentration is the ERL criteria, which is the 10th percentile concentration of a contaminant represented by studies demonstrating adverse biological effects in the literature. Ecological effects are not likely to occur at contaminant concentrations below the ERL criterion. The criteria for rating sediment contaminants at individual sampling sites are shown in Table 4.

Sediment contaminant availability or organic enrichment can be altered in areas where there is considerable deposition of organic matter. Sediment toxicity from organic matter is assessed by measuring TOC. The criteria for rating TOC for individual sampling sites are shown in Table 4.

After sediment contaminants and sediment TOC were assessed for a given site, the sediment quality index rating was calculated for the site and park based on these three indicators. The sediment quality index was rated good to poor for each site using the criteria shown in Table 4.

**Table 3.** Sediment contaminant guidance values from Long et al. (1995). Effects Range Low (ERL) thresholds are determined for each chemical as the 10th percentile in a database of ascending concentrations associated with biological effects. Effects Range Median (ERM) thresholds are determined for each chemical as the 50th percentile (median) in a database of ascending concentrations associated with adverse biological effects.

| Contaminant | ERL | ERM |
|---|---|---|
| **Metals (ppm)[a]** | | |
| Arsenic | 8.2 | 70 |
| Cadmium | 1.2 | 9.6 |
| Chromium | 81 | 370 |
| Copper | 37 | 270 |
| Lead | 46.7 | 218 |
| Mercury | 0.15 | 0.71 |
| Nickel | 20.9 | 51.6 |
| Silver | 1 | 3.7 |
| Zinc | 150 | 410 |
| **Organics (ppb)[b]** | | |
| Acenaphthene | 16 | 500 |
| Acenapthylene | 44 | 640 |
| Anthracene | 85.3 | 1,100 |
| Flourene | 19 | 540 |
| 2-Methyl napthalene | 70 | 670 |
| Napthalene | 160 | 2,100 |
| Phenanthrene | 240 | 1,500 |
| Benz(a)anthracene | 261 | 1,600 |
| Benzo(a)pyrene | 430 | 1,600 |
| Chrysene | 384 | 2,800 |
| Dibenzo(a,h)anthracene | 63.4 | 260 |
| Fluoranthene | 600 | 5,100 |
| Pyrene | 665 | 2,600 |
| Low molecular weight PAH | 552 | 3,160 |
| High molecular weight PAH | 1,700 | 9,600 |
| Total PAHs | 4,020 | 44,800 |
| 4,4'-DDE | 2.2 | 27 |
| Total DDT | 1.6 | 46.1 |
| Total PCBs | 22.7 | 180 |

[a] Units are ug/g dry sediment, equivalent to ppm.
[b] Units are ng/g dry sediment, equivalent to ppb.

**Table 4.** Condition criteria for sediment contaminants.

| Rating | Sediment Contaminants Rating (SC) | % Total Organic Carbon (TOC) | Site Sediment-Quality Index (SQI) | Park Sediment-Quality Index |
|---|---|---|---|---|
| Good | No ERM concentrations are exceeded and less than five ERL concentrations are exceeded. | < 2% | TOC is good and Sediment Contaminants Rating is good. | Less than 5% of the sites are rated in *Poor* condition and less than 50% of the sites are rated in combined *Poor* and *Fair* condition. |
| Fair | Five or more ERL concentrations are exceeded. | 2% – 5% | TOC is fair or Sediment Contaminants Rating is fair. | 5% to 15% of sites are in *Poor* condition, or more than 50% of sites are in combined *Poor* and *Fair* condition. |
| Poor | An ERM concentration is exceeded for one or more contaminants | > 5% | TOC is poor or Sediment Contaminants Indicator is poor. | More than 15% of sites are in *Poor* condition |

# Water-Quality Condition Assessments

Figures 3–7 show maps illustrating the spatial distribution of sampling sites and the corresponding ratings for water-clarity, chlorophyll *a*, total dissolved nitrogen, total dissolved phosphorus, and dissolved oxygen based on each parameter's corresponding condition category. Figure 9 shows a water-quality conditions summary for the Seashores. Data used to create maps and graphs are presented in Table 5.

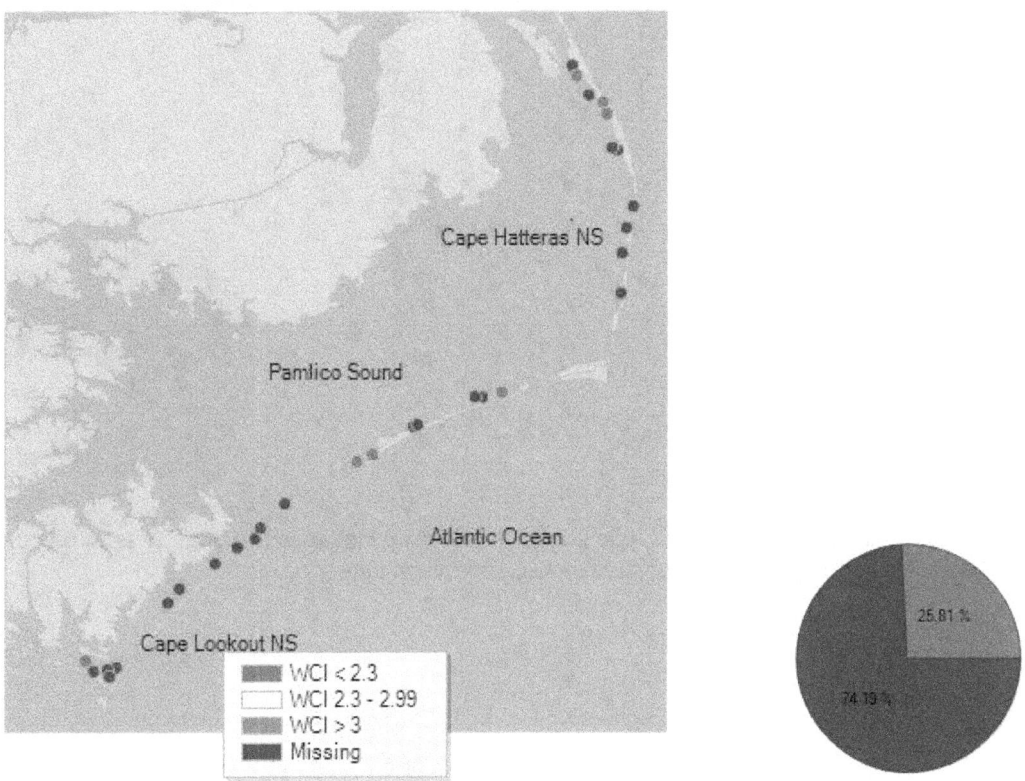

**Figure 3.** Water-clarity index (*WCI*) based on light attenuation estimates at sampling sites at Cape Lookout and Cape Hatteras National Seashores during July 2010. Graph shows the percentage of sites in each condition category. Missing data indicate places where the water-clarity index could not be calculated due to limited water depth.

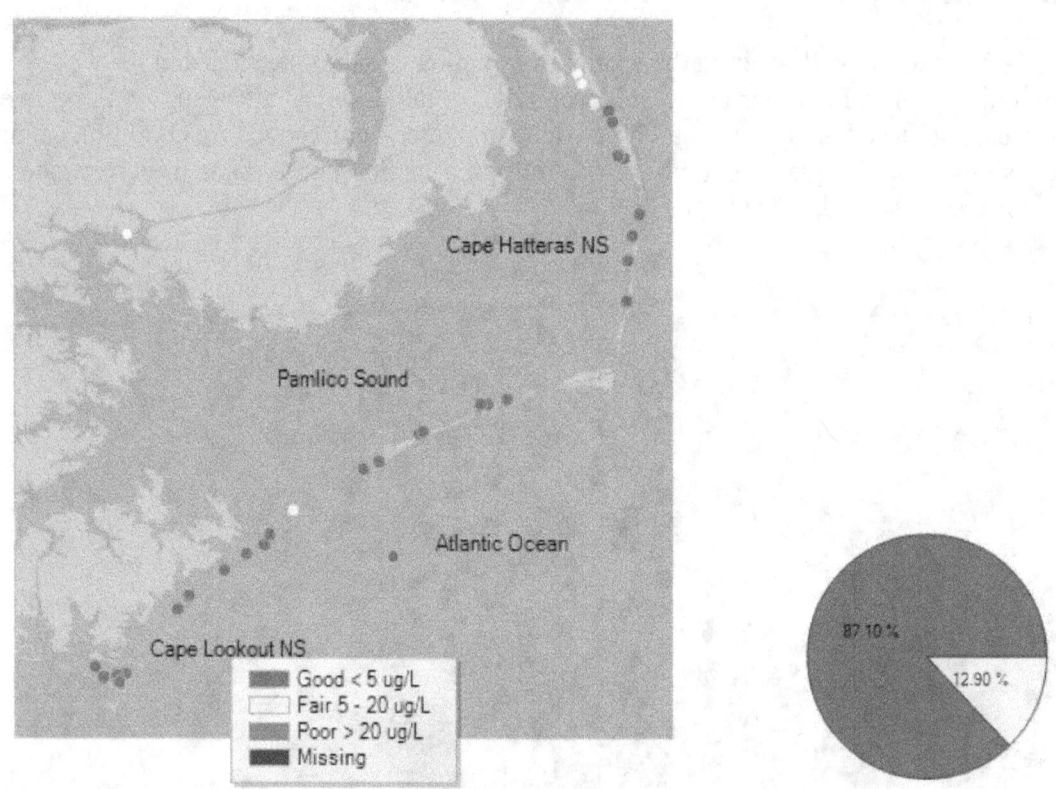

**Figure 4.** Chlorophyll a concentrations at Cape Lookout and Cape Hatteras National Seashores during July 2010. Graph shows the percentage of sites in each condition category.

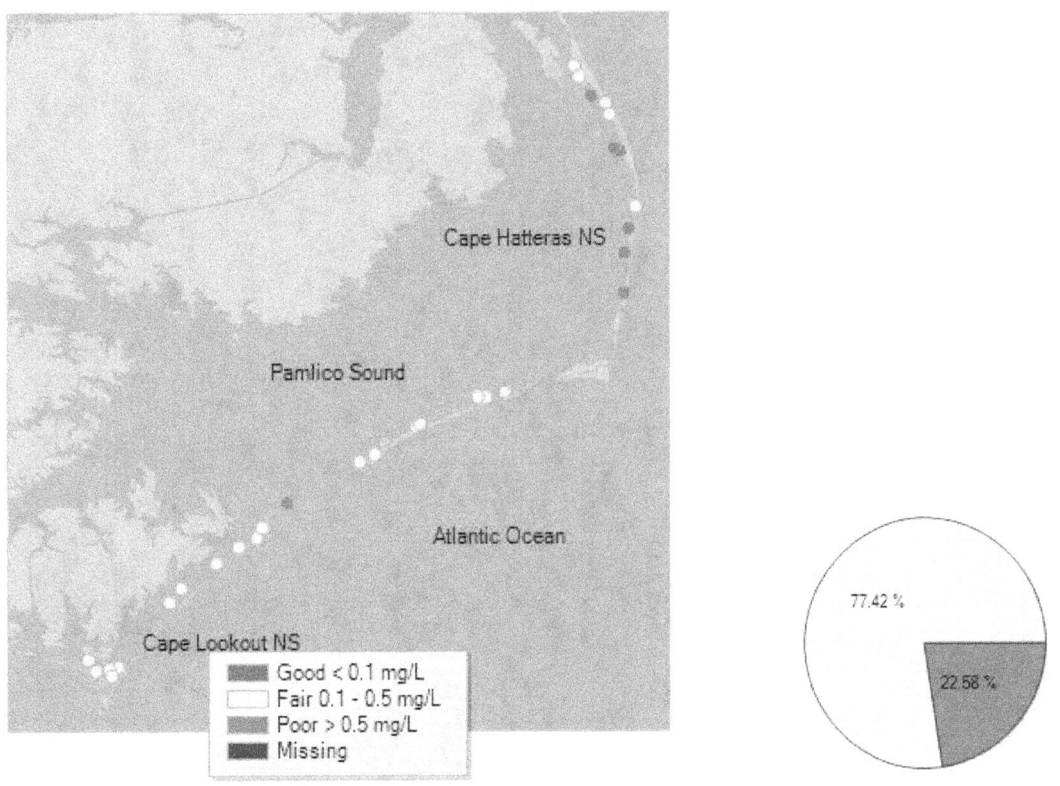

**Figure 5.** Total dissolved nitrogen (TDN) concentrations at Cape Lookout and Cape Hatteras National Seashores during July 2010. Graph shows percentage of sites in each condition category.

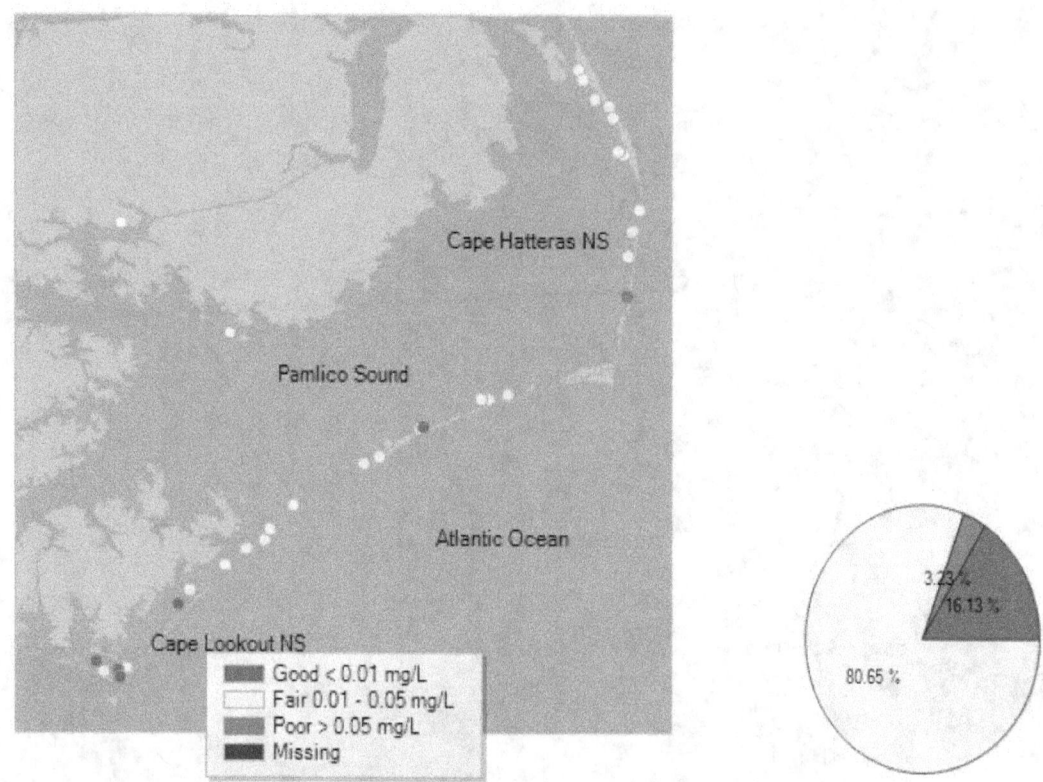

**Figure 6.** Total dissolved phosphorus (TDP) concentrations at Cape Lookout and Cape Hatteras National Seashores during July 2010. Graph shows percentage of sites in each condition category.

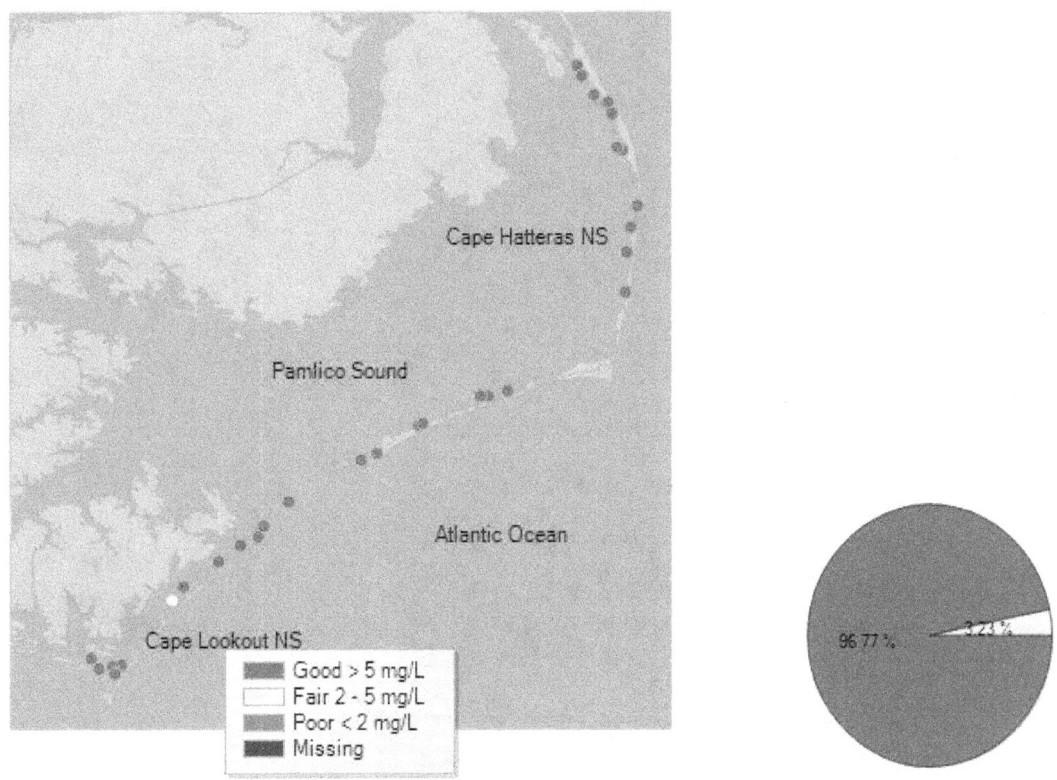

**Figure 7.** Dissolved oxygen concentrations at Cape Lookout and Cape Hatteras National Seashores during July 2010. Graph shows percentage of sites in each condition category.

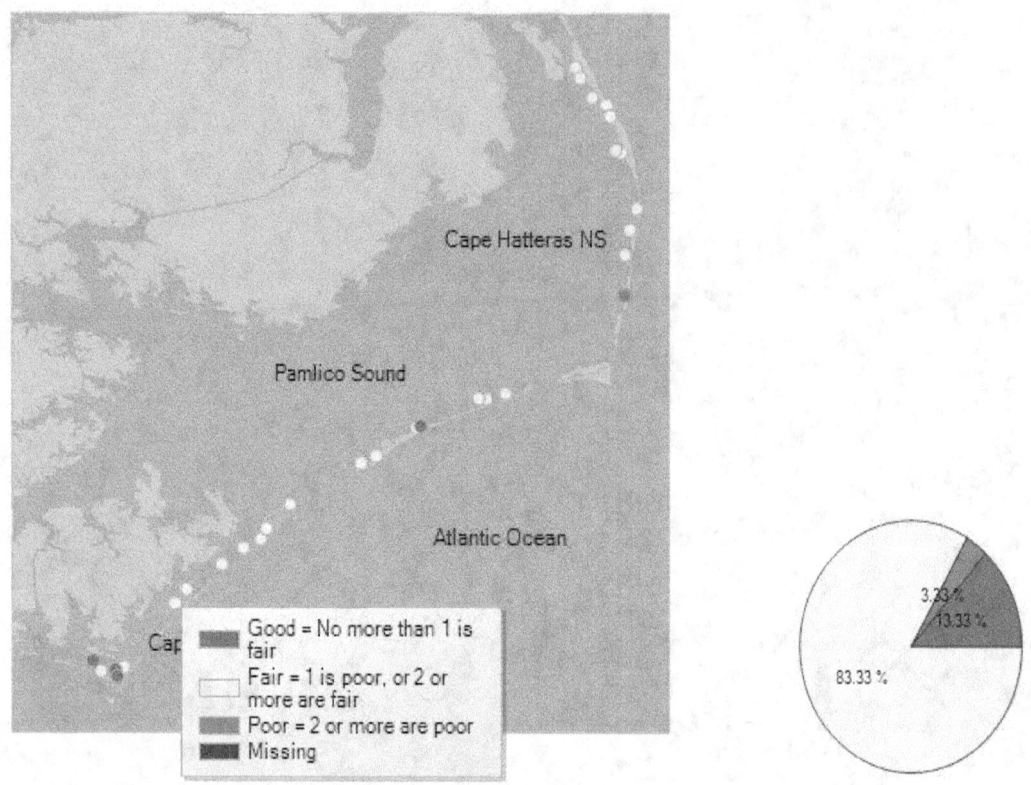

**Figure 8.** Summary assessment of water-quality conditions at Cape Lookout and Cape Hatteras National Seashores during July 2010. Assessment based on numbers of categorical ratings at each site for using the water-clarity index (*WCI*), chlorophyll *a*, total dissolved nitrogen, total dissolved phosphorus and dissolved oxygen measurements. Graph shows percentage of sites in each condition category.

# Sediment Condition Assessments

Figures 9, 10, and 11 are maps which show the spatial distribution of sampling sites and the corresponding ratings for sediment contamination based on a summary of data collected at each site. Inset graphs on each figure show the percentage of sites in each rating category. Data used to create maps and graphs are found in tables 6, 7, and 8. Sediment data were not collected at eight sites due to the presence of seagrass beds.

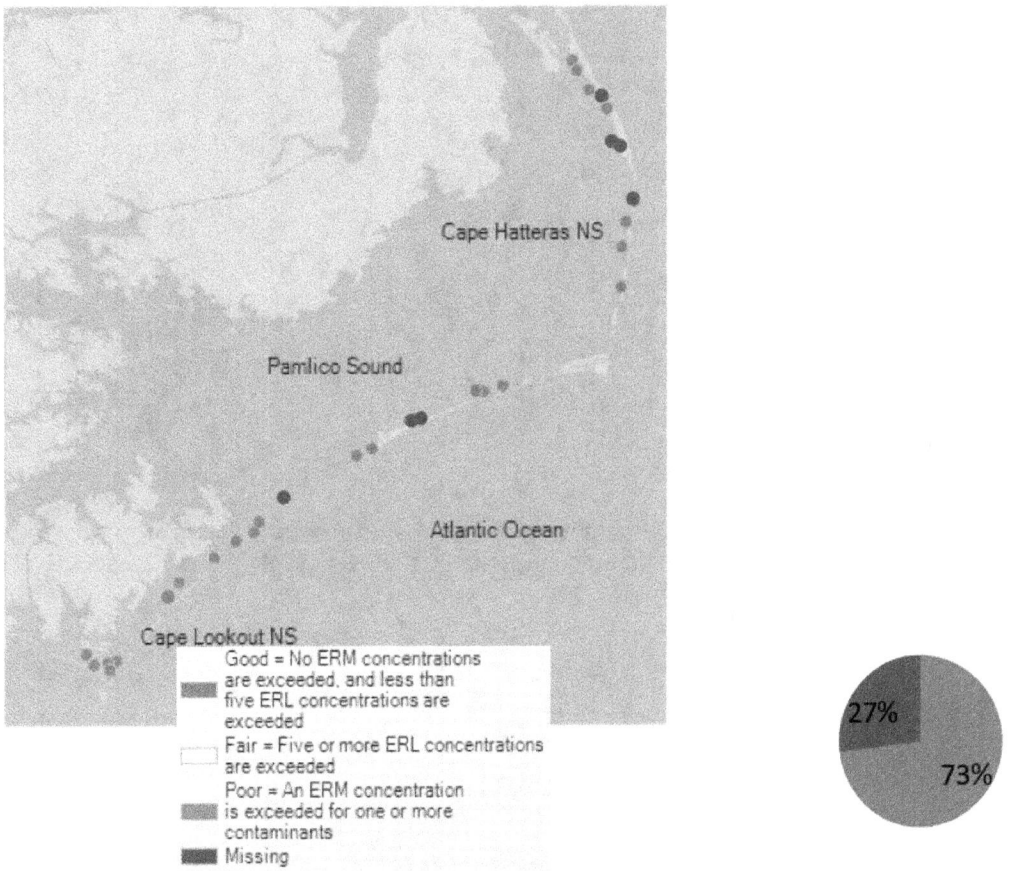

**Figure 9.** Sediment contaminant rating at Cape Lookout and Cape Hatteras National Seashores during July 2010. Assessment categories correspond to numbers of ERM and ERL concentrations exceeded at a site. Inset graph shows percentage of sites in each condition category.

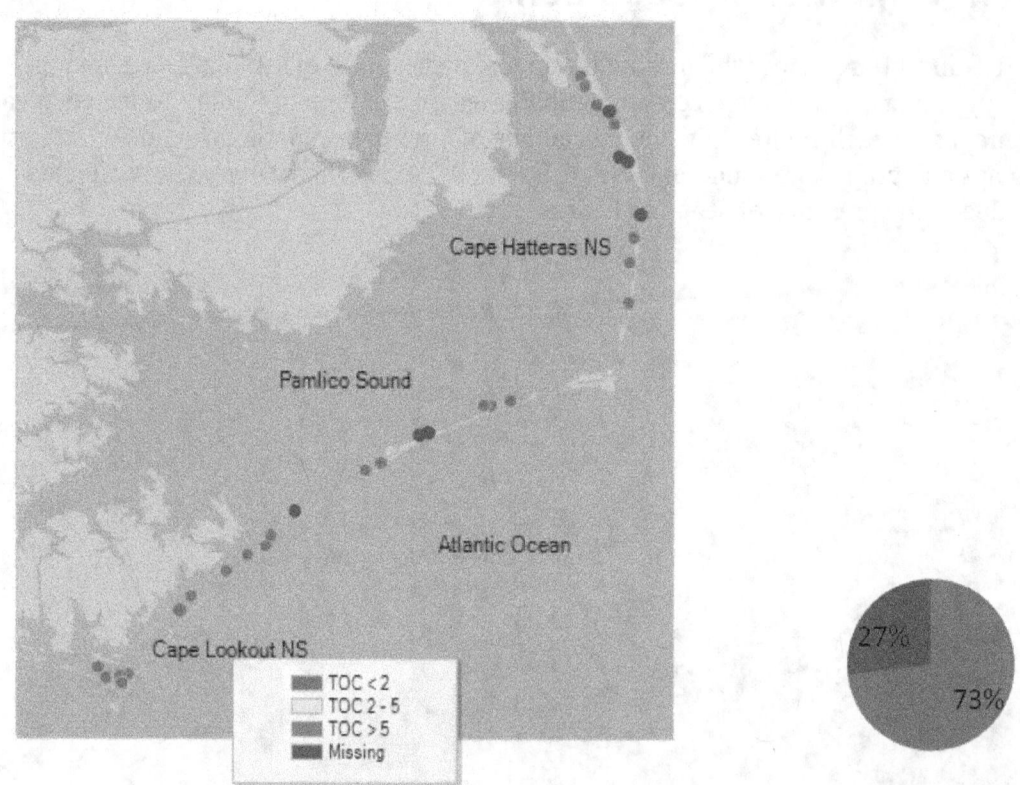

**Figure 10.** Total Organic Carbon (TOC) concentrations in sediments and condition ratings at Cape Lookout and Cape Hatteras National Seashores during July 2010. Inset graph shows percentage of sites in each condition category.

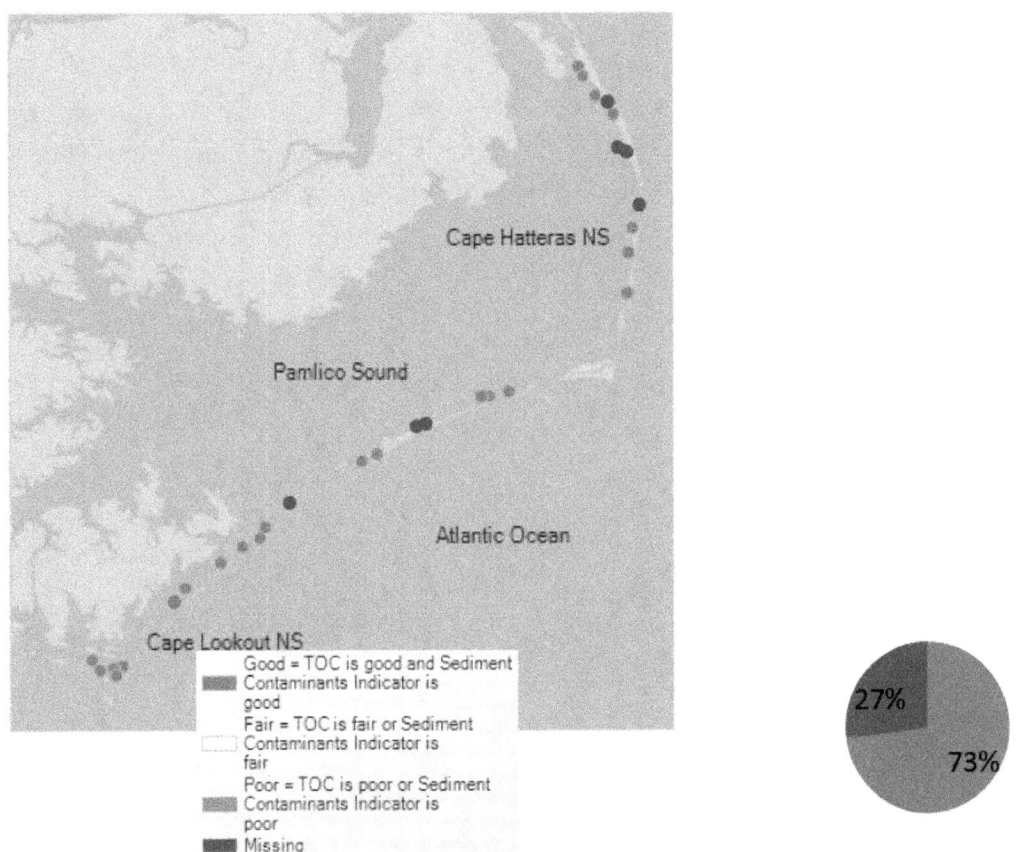

**Figure 11.** Sediment quality index ratings at Cape Lookout and Cape Hatteras National Seashores during July 2010. Inset graph shows percentage of sites in each condition category.

# Water-Quality Data

Table 5. Water-quality parameter values and assessment conditions for sites sampled at Cape Lookout and Cape Hatteras National Seashores during July 2010. Water Clarity Index (*k*) values were calculated using constant for estuarine water with naturally turbid conditions (Smith et al. 2006). Condition of assessed parameter from USEPA (2005). [Green, *good*; yellow, *fair;* and red, *poor*; blue, missing data; ug/L, micrograms per liter; mg/l, milligrams per liter]

| Station | Water Clarity Index (WCl) | Chlorophyll *a* (ug/L) | Total Dissolved Nitrogen (mg/L) | Total Dissolved Phosphorus (mg/L) | Dissolved Oxygen (mg/L) |
|---|---|---|---|---|---|
| **CAHA**CALO-01 | | 5.950 | 0.511 | 0.010 | 5.820 |
| **CAHA**CALO-02 | | 2.859 | 0.266 | 0.017 | 5.710 |
| **CAHA**CALO-05 | 0.495 | 2.429 | 0.148 | 0.011 | 6.670 |
| **CAHA**CALO-06 | | 4.220 | 0.544 | 0.233 | 6.130 |
| **CAHA**CALO-09 | | 2.307 | 0.564 | 0.011 | 9.910 |
| **CAHA**CALO-10 | 0.667 | 2.571 | 0.373 | 0.013 | 5.390 |
| **CAHA**CALO-14 | | 1.944 | 0.464 | 0.010 | 6.220 |
| **CAHA**CALO-17 | 0.588 | 1.180 | 0.156 | 0.011 | 6.410 |
| **CAHA**CALO-18 | | 3.172 | 0.596 | 0.013 | 6.340 |
| **CAHA**CALO-21 | | 3.401 | 0.520 | 0.010 | 6.890 |
| **CAHA**CALO-29 | | 1.982 | 0.506 | 0.011 | 9.680 |
| **CAHA**CALO-ALT-03 | | 14.493 | 0.335 | 0.010 | 6.890 |
| **CAHA**CALO-ALT-07 | | 4.539 | 0.475 | 0.016 | 5.520 |
| **CAHA**CALO-ALT-08 | 0.685 | 3.568 | 0.266 | 0.019 | 6.550 |
| **CAHA**CALO-ALT-19 | 1.053 | 18.940 | 0.309 | 0.013 | 7.310 |
| **CAHA**CALO-ALT-24 | | 2.571 | 0.496 | 0.008 | 8.180 |
| **CAHA**CALO-ALT-27 | | 3.165 | 0.287 | 0.016 | 5.410 |
| CAHA**CALO**-03 | | 7.115 | 0.618 | 0.012 | 5.620 |
| CAHA**CALO**-04 | | 1.371 | 0.159 | 0.012 | 6.260 |
| CAHA**CALO**-08 | | 0.849 | 0.314 | 0.011 | 7.180 |
| CAHA**CALO**-12 | | 1.168 | 0.259 | 0.008 | 4.410 |
| CAHA**CALO**-20 | | 0.577 | 0.160 | 0.009 | 6.680 |
| CAHA**CALO**-26 | | 2.887 | 0.191 | 0.011 | 5.150 |
| CAHA**CALO**-ALT-02 | 0.386 | 1.652 | 0.177 | 0.008 | 6.620 |
| CAHA**CALO**-ALT-05 | 0.585 | 3.370 | 0.255 | 0.016 | 6.780 |
| CAHA**CALO**-ALT-06 | | 0.584 | 0.139 | 0.007 | 6.060 |
| CAHA**CALO**-ALT-10 | | 1.969 | 0.288 | 0.011 | 5.690 |
| CAHA**CALO**-ALT-12 | | 3.228 | 0.443 | 0.011 | 9.230 |
| CAHA**CALO**-ALT-17 | | 2.915 | 0.408 | 0.013 | 8.090 |
| CAHA**CALO**-ALT-28 | | 1.869 | 0.194 | 0.012 | 7.230 |

# Sediment-Quality Data

**Table 6.** Concentrations of select metals (in ppm) for sites sampled at Cape Lookout and Cape Hatteras National Seashores during July 2010. Condition of assessed constituent from Long et al. (1995). [Green, *good*; yellow, *fair*; red, *poor*; —, value not reported, below the detection limit; *, estimated value, used in condition assessment summaries]

| Station | Arsenic | Cadmium | Chromium | Copper | Lead | Mercury | Nickel | Silver | Zinc |
|---------|---------|---------|----------|--------|------|---------|--------|--------|------|
| CAHACALO-01 | - | 0.38* | 6.76 | - | - | 2.27 | - | 11.5 | - |
| CAHACALO-02 | 6.68* | 0.412* | 2.94 | - | - | 0.527 | - | 3.4* | 6.68* |
| CAHACALO-04 | - | 0.919 | 4.18 | - | - | 1.31 | - | 5.47 | - |
| CAHACALO-06 | - | 0.438* | 2.15 | - | - | 0.557* | - | 4.36* | - |
| CAHACALO-08 | - | 0.956 | 6.00 | - | - | 1.11 | - | 7.78 | - |
| CAHACALO-10 | - | 0.448* | 5.40 | - | - | 1.50 | - | 7.11 | - |
| CAHACALO-12 | - | 0.962 | 4.41 | - | - | - | - | 5.6 | - |
| CAHACALO-17 | - | 0.487* | 2.46 | - | - | 0.892* | - | 5.01 | - |
| CAHACALO-20 | - | 1.030 | 9.45 | - | - | 1.97 | - | 10.8 | - |
| CAHACALO-21 | - | 0.305* | 6.60 | - | - | 1.69 | - | 11.0 | - |
| CAHACALO-26 | - | 0.382 | 5.94 | - | - | 1.34 | - | 7.1 | - |
| CAHACALO-ALT-02 | - | 1.080 | 10.70 | - | - | 3.25 | - | 14.7 | - |
| CAHACALO-ALT-03 | - | 0.456* | 3.10 | - | - | 1.04 | - | 4.95* | - |
| CAHACALO-ALT-05 | - | 0.428 | 3.36 | - | - | 0.792 | - | 4.96 | - |
| CAHACALO-ALT-06 | - | 1.010 | 4.51 | - | - | - | - | 5.72 | - |
| CAHACALO-ALT-07 | - | 0.374* | 5.09 | - | - | 1.40 | - | 8.51 | - |
| CAHACALO-ALT-10 | - | 0.396 | 5.64 | - | - | 1.42 | - | 7.2 | - |
| CAHACALO-ALT-12 | - | 0.284 | 6.71 | - | - | 1.16 | - | 10.6 | - |
| CAHACALO-ALT-17 | - | 0.401 | 3.64 | - | - | 0.87 | - | 4.53 | - |
| CAHACALO-ALT-19 | - | 0.347* | 6.89 | - | - | 2.19 | - | 10.4 | - |
| CAHACALO-ALT-27 | - | 0.436* | 5.10 | - | - | 1.45 | - | 7.46 | - |
| CAHACALO-ALT-28 | - | 0.329 | 7.81 | - | - | 1.64 | - | 10.6 | - |

**Table 7.** Organic contaminant concentrations (in ppb) and totals for select classes of compounds for sites sampled at Cape Lookout and Cape Hatteras National Seashores during July 2010. [Blue, missing data; green, good; yellow, fair; red, poor; —, value not reported, below the detection limit]

| Station | 2-Methylnaphthalene | 4,4'-DDE | Acenaphthene | Acenaphthylene | Anthracene | Benz[a]anthracene | Benzo[a]pyrene | Chrysene | Dibenz[a,h]anthracene | Fluoranthene | Fluorene | Naphthalene | Phenanthrene | Pyrene | Total DDT | High molecular weight PAH | Low molecular weight PAH | Total PAHs | Total PCBs |
|---|---|---|---|---|---|---|---|---|---|---|---|---|---|---|---|---|---|---|---|
| CAHACALO-01 | - | - | - | - | - | - | - | - | - | - | - | - | - | - | 0 | 0 | 0 | 0 | 0 |
| CAHACALO-02 | - | - | - | - | - | - | - | - | - | - | - | - | - | - | 0 | 0 | 0 | 0 | 0 |
| CAHACALO-04 | - | - | - | - | - | - | - | - | - | - | - | - | - | - | 0 | 0 | 0 | 0 | 0 |
| CAHACALO-06 | - | - | - | - | - | - | - | - | - | - | - | - | - | - | 0 | 0 | 0 | 0 | 0 |
| CAHACALO-08 | - | - | - | - | - | - | - | - | - | - | - | - | - | - | 0 | 0 | 0 | 0 | 0 |
| CAHACALO-10 | - | - | - | - | - | - | - | - | - | - | - | - | - | - | 0 | 0 | 0 | 0 | 0 |
| CAHACALO-12 | - | - | - | - | - | - | - | - | - | - | - | - | - | - | 0 | 0 | 0 | 0 | 0 |
| CAHACALO-17 | - | - | - | - | - | - | - | - | - | - | - | - | - | - | 0 | 0 | 0 | 0 | 0 |
| CAHACALO-20 | - | - | - | - | - | - | - | - | - | - | - | - | - | - | 0 | 0 | 0 | 0 | 0 |
| CAHACALO-21 | - | - | - | - | - | - | - | - | - | - | - | - | - | - | 0 | 0 | 0 | 0 | 0 |
| CAHACALO-26 | - | - | - | - | - | - | - | - | - | - | - | - | - | - | 0 | 0 | 0 | 0 | 0 |
| CAHACALO-ALT-02 | - | - | - | - | - | - | - | - | - | - | - | - | - | - | 0 | 0 | 0 | 0 | 0 |
| CAHACALO-ALT-03 | - | - | - | - | - | - | - | - | - | - | - | - | - | - | 0 | 0 | 0 | 0 | 0 |
| CAHACALO-ALT-05 | - | - | - | - | - | - | - | - | - | - | - | - | - | - | 0 | 0 | 0 | 0 | 0 |
| CAHACALO-ALT-06 | - | - | - | - | - | - | - | - | - | - | - | - | - | - | 0 | 0 | 0 | 0 | 0 |
| CAHACALO-ALT-07 | - | - | - | - | - | - | - | - | - | - | - | - | - | - | 0 | 0 | 0 | 0 | 0 |
| CAHACALO-ALT-10 | - | - | - | - | - | - | - | - | - | - | - | - | - | - | 0 | 0 | 0 | 0 | 0 |
| CAHACALO-ALT-12 | - | - | - | - | - | - | - | - | - | - | - | - | - | - | 0 | 0 | 0 | 0 | 0 |
| CAHACALO-ALT-17 | - | - | - | - | - | - | - | - | - | - | - | - | - | - | 0 | 0 | 0 | 0 | 0 |
| CAHACALO-ALT-19 | - | - | - | - | - | - | - | - | - | - | - | - | - | - | 0 | 0 | 0 | 0 | 0 |
| CAHACALO-ALT-27 | - | - | - | - | - | - | - | - | - | - | - | - | - | - | 0 | 0 | 0 | 0 | 0 |
| CAHACALO-ALT-28 | - | - | - | - | - | - | - | - | - | - | - | - | - | - | 0 | 0 | 0 | 0 | 0 |

**Table 8.** Sediment contaminant rating, total organic carbon (TOC), and Sediment Quality Index (SQI) rating for sites sampled at Cape Lookout and Cape Hatteras National Seashores during July 2010. [Green, *good*; yellow, *fair*; red, *poor*; blue, missing data]

| Station | Sediment Contaminant Rating | Total Organic Carbon (%) | Sediment Quality Index |
|---------|------------------------------|---------------------------|------------------------|
| CAHACALO-01 | Good | 0.108 | Good |
| CAHACALO-02 | Good | 0.0637 | Good |
| CAHACALO-04 | Good | 0.0835 | Good |
| CAHACALO-06 | Good | 0.0584 | Good |
| CAHACALO-08 | Good | 0.143 | Good |
| CAHACALO-10 | Good | 0.125 | Good |
| CAHACALO-12 | Good | 0.0722 | Good |
| CAHACALO-17 | Good | 0.0103 | Good |
| CAHACALO-20 | Good | 0.113 | Good |
| CAHACALO-21 | Good | 0.053 | Good |
| CAHACALO-26 | Good | 0.076 | Good |
| CAHACALO-ALT-02 | Good | 0.144 | Good |
| CAHACALO-ALT-03 | Good | 0.106 | Good |
| CAHACALO-ALT-05 | Good | 0.026 | Good |
| CAHACALO-ALT-06 | Good | 0.0823 | Good |
| CAHACALO-ALT-07 | Good | 0.0613 | Good |
| CAHACALO-ALT-10 | Good | 0.0747 | Good |
| CAHACALO-ALT-12 | Good | 0.0792 | Good |
| CAHACALO-ALT-17 | Good | 0.0711 | Good |
| CAHACALO-ALT-19 | Good | 0.146 | Good |
| CAHACALO-ALT-27 | Good | 0.0777 | Good |
| CAHACALO-ALT-28 | Good | 0.0847 | Good |

# Literature Cited

DeVivo, J. C., C. J. Wright, M. W. Byrne, E. DiDonato, and T. Curtis. 2008. Vital signs monitoring in the Southeast Coast Inventory & Monitoring Network. Natural Resource Report NPS/SECN/NRR—2008/061. National Park Service, Fort Collins, Colorado.

DeVivo, J. C., E. M. DiDonato, C. J. Wright, Y. Li, and M. B. Gregory, Assessment of estuarine water and sediment quality in the Southeast Coast Network, *in review.*

Freeman, D., Jr. 1988. An examination of the effects of mechanical harvesting of clams in North Carolina. North Carolina Department of Natural Resources and Community Development, Division of Marine Fisheries, Morehead City, N.C.

Holland, A. F., D. M. Sanger, C. P. Gawle, S. B. Lerberg, M. S. Santiago, G. H. M. Riekerk, L. E. Zimmerman, and G. I. Scott. 2004. Linkages between tidal creek ecosystems and the landscape and demographic attributes of their wetlands. Journal of Experimental Marine Biology and Ecology 298: 151-178.

Lerberg, S. B., A. F. Holland, and D. Sanger. 2000. Responses of tidal creek macrobenthic communities to the effects of watershed development. Estuaries 23(6): 838-853.

Long, E. R., D. D. MacDonald, S. L. Smith, and F. D. Calder. 1995. Incidence of adverse biological effects within ranges of chemical concentrations in marine and estuarine sediments. Environmental Management 19(1): 81–97.

Mallin, Michael A. V. L. Johnson, and M. R. McIver. 2004. Assessment of Coastal Water Resources and Watershed Conditions in Cape Lookout National Seashore North Carolina. Technical Report NPS/NRWRD/NRTR-2004/322.

Smith Lee M., V. D. Engle and J. K. Summers. 2006. Assessing water clarity as a component of water quality in the Gulf of Mexico estuaries. Environmental Monitoring and Assessment. 115: 291-305.

Stevens, D. L., Jr. 1997. Variable density grid-based sampling designs for continuous spatial populations. Envirometrics 8: 167-195.

Stevens, D. L., Jr. and A. R. Olsen. 1999. Spatially restricted surveys over time for aquatic resources. Journal of Agricultural, Biological and Environmental Statistics 4: 415-428.

Stevens, D. and A. R. Olsen. 2004. Spatially balanced sampling of natural resources. Journal of the American Statistical Association 99: 262-278.

U.S. EPA. 2001. Environmental Monitoring and Assessment Program (EMAP). National Coastal Assessment Quality Assurance Project Plan 2001 – 2004. United States Environmental Protection Agency, Office of Research and Development, National Health and Environmental Effects Research Laboratory, Gulf Ecology Division, Gulf Breeze, FL. EPA/620/R-01/002.

U.S. EPA. 2005. National Coastal Condition Report II. EPA-620/R-03/002. Office of Research and Development and Office of Water, Washington, D.C., USA.